CW00551494

FREDDIE MERCURY

Lines to Live By

POP PRESS

Pop Press, an imprint of Ebury Publishing
20 Vauxhall Bridge Road
London SW1V 2SA

Pop Press is part of the Penguin Random House group of companies
whose addresses can be found at global.penguinrandomhouse.com

Copyright © Pop Press 2024

First published by Pop Press in 2024

Design: Ed Pickford
Text: Liz Marvin
Illustrations: Ollie Mann

www.penguin.co.uk

A CIP catalogue record for this book is available from the British Library

ISBN 9781529933321

Typeset in 9/14.3pt Walbaum by Jouve (UK), Milton Keynes
Printed and bound in Great Britain by Clays Ltd, Elcograf S.p.A.

The authorised representative in the EEA is Penguin Random House
Ireland, Morrison Chambers, 32 Nassau Street, Dublin D02 YH68

Penguin Random House is committed to a sustainable future
for our business, our readers and our planet. This book is made
from Forest Stewardship Council® certified paper.

Contents

Introduction 1

Music 9

Performing 23

Success............................. 41

Friendship........................57

Style 73

Confidence 91

Philosophy 101

Oh god, dear! Let them think
what they want!

Introduction

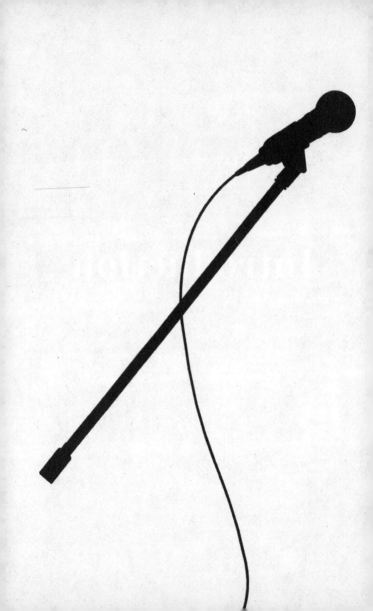

Live Like Freddie

The man the world came to know and love as Freddie Mercury chose his own name, created his identity and became one of music's most iconic performers. Born in Zanzibar to Indian Parsi parents, as the frontman of Queen, Freddie defied rock conventions and wrote songs that blended musical styles and showcased his incredible four-octave range.

Freddie was known for his flamboyant style but offstage, many who knew him reflected that he could be shy. In interviews, he could be witty and arch, but also quietly spoken and reflective. His refusal to be defined by others is as much part of his legacy as his incredible talent for performing. The songs he wrote with his friends and bandmates Brian May, John Deacon and Roger Taylor have travelled around the world and Freddie Mercury has become a hero to many.

When Freddie died of AIDS-related complications on 24 November 1991, the world lost an artist and a man who was utterly unique. In perhaps the final act of Mercury mystique, Freddie asked to be cremated and for his best friend and one-time fiancée Mary Austin to never disclose where she scattered his ashes. The location remains unknown.

Freddie Mercury may have been one of a kind, but we can all be inspired his passion for life and music, his live-for-the-moment philosophy and his inability to be anyone but himself . . .

Believe in your vision

Freddie and Queen often came in for criticism for taking their music in a different direction – whether that was opera or disco. But Freddie didn't care. For him, evolution was everything and one of the worst things you could do is to stay still.

Never apologise, never explain

Freddie never hid who he was but he also never came out publicly as gay or bisexual. He had no interest in labels other people might want to put on him and generally dismissed questions from pushy journalists with a witty quip. He believed that everyone should have the right to live how they wish and no one owes anyone else an explanation.

Be fabulous

Freddie's dazzling stage outfits and his incredible sense of style defined the look of rock music in the seventies and eighties, still inspiring musicians and designers to this day. He dressed for himself and to look great while performing, though he never took it too seriously. The most important thing for him was to feel fabulous and express himself. What other people think is irrelevant.

Celebrate success

Queen's songs are staples of the rock music cannon, their albums went multi-platinum and Freddie often strode out onstage in front of audiences of hundreds of thousands. For Freddie, confidence was key and he didn't see the point in pretending to be humble. He always kept his sense of humour and loved joking with journalists about how much money he had.

Live in the moment

For Freddie, it was all about embracing the moment. A philosophy which probably contributed to making him such a mesmerising performer. He often said that he had no interest in

his legacy or what would happen in the future,
because he was enjoying everything too much in
the now.

Music

'I'm just a musical prostitute, dear.'

'*Music is for everybody,
it's an international
language. Music
is limitless.*'

'A song can mean anything. But I'm a true romantic and a very loving person, and I think that comes out in my songs.'

'YOU'RE NOT going to ask me to interpret "Bohemian Rhapsody", are you?'

'I am the artistic
leader of the group,
I say what can and
cannot be done on an
LP and we sometimes
get endless discussions
about that, but in
hindsight, I'm right.'

'When they stop buying our records, then I'll say goodbye and do something else. Become an escape artist or something.'

'I just like people
to put their own
interpretation on my
songs. Really, they
are just like little
fairy stories.'

'If I can write a
good song, that's
enough. The gadgets
come later.'

'We like to think the
name stands for
something majestic.
Something with a
lot of excitement
and mystique.'

'Actually, it's just a name.'

'I'm a frontman, just a singer. Brian's the musician. I leave the virtuosity to him.'

'In the studio we use all the techniques available because they are there.'

Performing

'A concert is not a live rendition of our album. It's a theatrical event.'

'I'm very frivolous and
I like to enjoy myself.
And what better way
than on stage in front
of 300,000 people?'

'It's my job to make
sure people have a
good time. That's
part of my duty. It's
all to do with feeling
in control.'

'I'm going to shatter some illusions.'

*'I change when
I walk out on stage.'*

'Jimi Hendrix is very important. He's my idol. He sort of epitomises, from his presentation onstage, the whole works of a rock star.'

*'I'm a bit ham, really.
I just get on that
stage and do it.'*

'I think it's going to be chaotic [on stage]. It has to be. I mean, we're not all wonderfully well-behaved kids, are we . . .?'

'*People were quite amazed at the fact that we could fool around, drag up and still be good musicians.*'

'Basically, we are a very live act.'

*'What you see onstage
is me offstage, too.
Just not as dramatic.'*

'It's a great kick to be able to play to sold-out halls again night after night. As an artist, that is the greatest reward you can get for your creative achievements.'

'Every time I see [the audience] empathise with our music, a warm feeling goes through me.'

'I'm quite happy
being the lead poseur
in Queen.'

*'All this is a pretence.
It's fun.'*

Success

'*I always knew I was a star. And now, the rest of the world seems to agree with me.*'

'Some people can take second best, but I can't.'

Interviewer: What about coping with wealth? That's one thing that a lot of musicians find very difficult.

Freddie: I cope very well, actually. I spend it.

'When the wheels are turning, you can't sit back.'

'You've got to have
some kind of goal —
to get bigger is one.'

'Oh, we love the money. If they say they don't like the money, they're talking out of their ass.'

'New bands must face
strong competition.
That's how you get
to anything.'

'I can bring the whip
down and show them
who's in control.'

'They wanted four
wholesome lads to
play some nice music.
Now I'd like to
buy up the entire
continent and install
myself as president.'

Freddie on America

'If my music makes people happy, that's a wonderful thing.'

*'At the moment,
darling, I'm smiling
from my arse
to elbow!'*

'Even if it's just an hour of their lives, if I can make [people] feel lucky or make them feel good, or bring a smile to a sour face, that to me is worthwhile.'

'I don't want to go
down in history
worried about,
"My god, I hope they
realise that, after
I'm dead, I've created
something or I was
something." I've been
having fun.'

Friendship

'He lived for the band – it was his family.'

Brian May on Freddie

'I still miss him. He was my best friend, my best man. We shared so much and I owe so much to him.'

Roger Taylor on Freddie

'When you are highly strung and take your work seriously, you're bound to appear difficult to the outside world.'

'Go on, let the girl
have some fun.'

*Freddie on taking
Lady Diana Spencer
to a gay bar*

'I always felt that you
have to be the captain
of the ship every time
there is any kind of
gathering or whatever.
I was working so
hard, performing
for everybody.'

'There are no less
important people . . .
everyone plays a
leading role in
the group.'

'We address our differences quite openly and when I say something, and someone doesn't like it – it's bullshit.'

'We argue about everything — constantly. But then we've all got massive egos so we're bound to. Really though, we get on very well.'

'I'm possessed by love – but isn't everybody?'

'I don't want to [go to heaven]. Hell's much better. Look at all the interesting people you're going to meet down there.'

'You own dogs, cats
own you.'

'This album is dedicated to my cat Jerry – also Tom, Oscar and Tiffany, and all the cat lovers across the universe – screw everybody else!'

'The only friend I've got is Mary [Austin], and I don't want anybody else. To me, she was my common-law wife. To me, it was a marriage. We believe in each other, that's enough for me.'

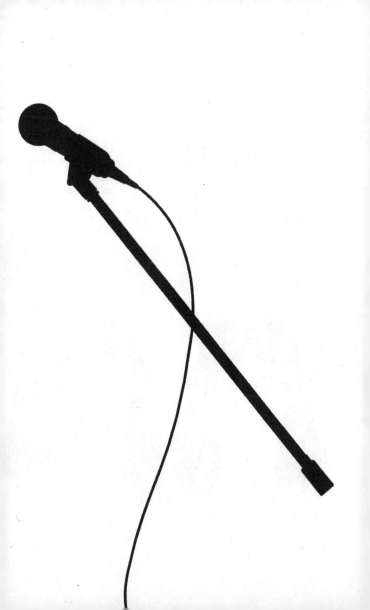

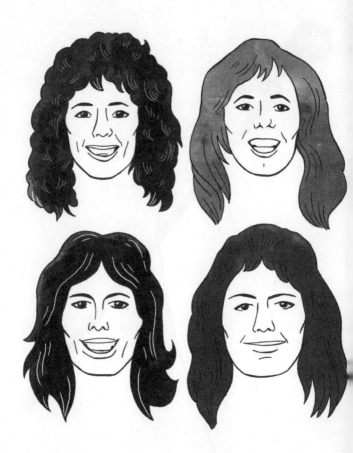

Style

*'I dress to kill,
but tastefully.'*

*'Dullness is
a disease.'*

'*Oh no, I never tie my own shoelaces! It's just not the thing done in rock and roll.*'

'One must always
have a sense of
impeccable style.'

'No, Mercury isn't my real name, dear. I changed it from Pluto.'

'Certainly I'm a flamboyant person. I like to live life. I certainly work hard for it, and I want to have a good time. Don't deny me that.'

'Whatever you say about me, don't make me sound boring.'

'The concept of Queen is to be regal and majestic. Glamour is a part of us and we want to be dandy.'

'Darling, I'm simply dripping with money! It may be vulgar, but it's wonderful.'

'I'm as gay as a daffodil, my dear!'

'Some of the things
I wear are over the
top. They have an
element of humour to
them, which I think
comes across.'

*'There seems to
be such a lot of
excitement missing
from the showbiz
world these days
and it's about time
something new
should happen.'*

'I am myself, unpredictable. I give what they expect of me, and I can also surprise with something out of the ordinary.'

'Lately I've been going in for simpler things. But don't worry, I haven't lost my spark.'

'We have to do some
of the old numbers as
well, but we've tried
to give them a bit of
a facelift. Actually,
I think it's the
musicians who could
probably use a
facelift.'

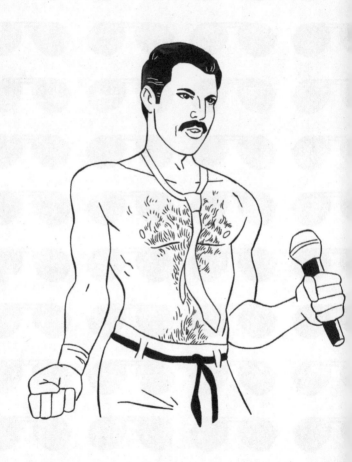

Confidence

'On the stage, he could be exactly who he wanted to be. There's something quite powerful about that, not really caring about people's perceptions.'

Rami Malek, on playing Freddie

'*I like to try everything once, and I'm not scared of the pitfalls.*'

'You have to have confidence in this business. It's USELESS saying you don't need it.'

'Stuff your criticism.'

'I'm not afraid to fall flat on my face.'

'When you take
your job seriously,
people in the biz
immediately think
you want to be
difficult. That is not
true. I am not a court
jester to be played
with, but a king.'

'It's up to you, in the
end ... You would be
amazed what the
human being can do.'

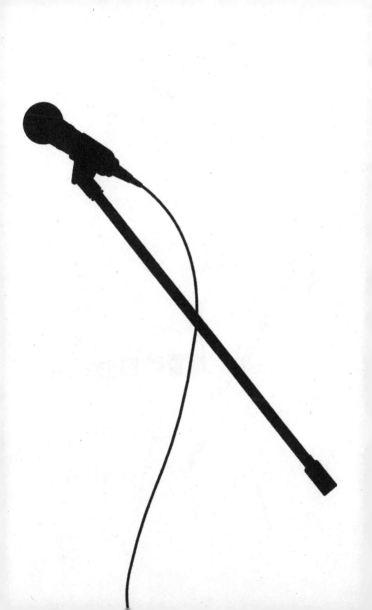

Philosophy

'*I just want to spend
my life doing
wonderful things.*'

'We don't consciously think about what's going to happen in a year's time. We're not that kind of group. Things just happen day to day and everything we do is at that very moment.'

'Just throw me in the lake when I go.'

'I'm not afraid to speak out, and say things that I want to do.'

'*I really believed that I'm not normal so I can't have a normal sort of life.*'

'The private life is up
to the individual.'

'Do I feel older now? Not really. I still have energy for ten and even the symbolic milestone of forty doesn't deter me. As long as parties are part of it, I will continue to find the life of a pop star very interesting.'

*'Don't get too serious
and too moody
about it.'*

'There's always some good you can get out of a situation.'

*'The sunshine makes
such a difference.'*

'I don't give a shit if they forget me to be honest, I really don't, because life is for living. In the meantime, I have been having fun.'

'I want to do
whatever my mind
says, whatever my
heart tells me to do.'

'*I'm quite a chameleon. I change, I have moods. I think it's a combination of a lot of sort of characters that make up a person.*'

'But people grow up,
don't they? I know
I have.'

'Because it's the music that matters, you've got to make sure there are key people around you, taking care of you.'

'*It is impossible to replace Freddie.*'

John Deacon

*'I won't be a rock star.
I will be a legend.'*

Acknowledgements

Epigraph from Evening News, 'In the Camp of Queen Freddie' (1980). Page 10 from Greatest Video Hits 2 'Musical Prostitute: Freddie Mercury Interview (1984). Page 11 from Ultimate Queen, 'The David Wigg Interview' (1979). Page 12 from Radio X, 'Freddie Mercury in his own words' (2023).Page 13 from Phonograph Record, 'Queen The New British Invasion' (Mitchell Cohen, 1976). Page 14 from Joepie, 'Freddie Mercury Looks Back' (1981). Page 15 from Greatest Video Hits (1984). Page 16 from NME, 'Queen' (Julie Webb, 1974). Page 17 from Off The Record (1984). Page 18 from Record Mirror, 'No limp wrists on this Queen' (Peter Harvey, 1973). Page 19 from The Journal, "Queen' Show Not All Theatrics' (Mary Campbell, 1974). Page 20 from Circus Magazine, 'Art v Life' (Stephen Ford, 1976). Page 21 from Record Mirror, 'Queen Back on the Throne' (Martin Thorpe, 1974). Page 24 from Circus, 'Queen Tapes', (1977). Page 25 from The Greatest Live, 'Episode 35' (2023). Page 26 from Gold, 'Freddie Mercury's scathing response to the UK Punk Movement revealed' (2023). Page 27 from Sounds, 'Mercury Rising' (John Ingham, 1976). Page 28 from The Voice of Fashion, 'Freddie Mercury Addressing the Audience' (Cynthia Green, 2019). Page 29 from Circus Magazine, 'Shopping for an Image in London' (Scott Cohen, 1975). Page 30 from Entertainment Tonight, 'Watch Freddie Mercury's Rare 1982 ET Interview' (2018). Page 31 from Louder Sound, "It's going to be chaotic' (Paul Brannigan, 2023). Page 32 from Queen Official, 'Queen on Air Interview – Freddie Mercury with Simon Bates (1985). Page 33 from Music Scene, 'Band of the Month' (1974). Page 34 from Circus Magazine, 'Art v Life' (Stephen Ford, 1976). Page 35 from Joepie, 'Freddie Mercury is Crowned' (1986). Page 36 from Joepie, 'Freddie Mercury is Crowned' (1986). Page 37 from Hit Parader, 'Queen' (Lester Bangs, 1977). Page 38 from The Express, 'Freddie Mercury'

ACKNOWLEDGEMENTS

(Minnie Wright, 2020). Page 42 from Parade, '75 Freddie Mercury Quotes to Celebrate the 30th Anniversary of the Legendary Freddie Mercury Tribute Concert' (Kai Green, 2022). Page 43 from The Daily Mail, 'The last days (and exuberantly wild life) of my friend Freddie Mercury' (David Wigg, 2021). Page 44-45 from Ultimate Queen, 'The David Wigg Interview' (1979). Page 46 from The Journal, "Queen' Show Not All Theatrics' (Mary Campbell, 1974). Page 47 from The Journal, "Queen' Show Not All Theatrics' (Mary Campbell, 1974). Page 48 from MTV News 'MTV News Interviews Freddie Mercury in 1984'. Page 49 from Pelo, 'We Like to Try Everything' (1985). Page 50 from Record Mirror, 'Blame it on Rio' (Robin Smith,1985). Page 51 from Record Mirror, 'Blame it on Rio' (Robin Smith,1985). Page 52 from The Solo Collection: The David Wigg Interviews 'Munich, 1984'. Page 53 from The Solo Collection: The David Wigg Interviews, 'Ibiza, 1987'. Page 54 from Huffington Post, 'Freddie Mercury Quotes: Remembering the Queen Frontman with 23 of His Best Lines' (Daniel Welsh, 2021). Page 58 from Brave Worlds, 'Queen Guitarist Brian May on Freddie Mercury' (2021). Page 59 from The Express, 'Roger Taylor: Deaf Metal' (Brigit Grant, 2011). Page 60 from Melody Maker, 'The Man Who Would Be Queen' (Ray Coleman, 1981). Page 61 from Tatler, 'When Freddie Mercury smuggled Princess Diana into a gay bar' (Hope Coke, 2020). Page 62 from Freddie Mercury, The Solo Collection: The David Wigg Interviews (1987). Page 63 from Musikexpress & Sounds, 'Freddie Mercury' (Steve Lake, 1984). Page 64 from Musikexpress & Sounds, 'Freddie Mercury' (Steve Lake, 1984). Page 65 from The Record Mirror, 'A Rendezvous at the opera' (Ray Fox-Cumming, 1975). Page 66 from The International Business Times, 'I Will be a legend' (Alicia Adejobi, 2016). Page 67 from The Show Must Go On, (Dir Christopher Bird and Simon Lupton, 2019). Page 68 from The Express, 'Freddie Mercury cuddled his favourite cat at the end' (Stefan Kyriazis, 2022). Page 69 from Sleeve Notes, 'Mr Bad Guy' (1985). Page 70 from The New York Post, 'Meet the woman a closeted Freddie Mercury fell in love with' (Dana Schuster, 2018). Page 74 from Pink News, '13 incredible, brave and bold queer moments from Freddie Mercury, the greatest showman of all time' (Josh Milton, 2023). Page 75 from Huffington Post, 'Freddie Mercury Quotes' (Daniel Welsh, 2021). Page 76 from Billboard, 'Freddie Mercury's 5 Sassiest Moments' (Starr Bowenbank, 2018). Page 77 from Jackie, 'The Queen of Arts' (1976). Page 78 from Melody Maker, 'The Queen Bee' (Caroline Coon, 1974). Page 79 NME, 'Interview with Freddie Mercury' (Tony Stewart, 1977). Page 80 from The Daily Mail, 'The last days (and exuberantly wild life) of my friend Freddie Mercury' (David Wigg, 2021). Page 81 from Circus Magazine, 'Shopping for an Image in London' (Scott Cohen, 1975). Page 82 from Q Magazine, 'Happy & Glorious' (Phil Sutcliffe, 1991). Page 83 from BBC.com 'Who was the real Freddie Mercury?' (Nick Levine, 2019). Page 84 from Mirabelle, 'Introducing Queen' (1973). Page 85 from Entertainment Tonight, 'Watch Freddie Mercury's Rare 1982 ET Interview' (2018). Page 85 from Mirabelle, 'Introducing Queen' (1973). Page 86 from Pelo, 'We Like to Try Everything' (1985). Page 87 from US, 'it's Hits May be 'Fat' but Queen is lean and mean' (Carl Arrington, 1979). Page 88 from Hit Parader, 'Queen' (Lester Bangs, 1977). Page 92 from Backstage, 'Rami Malek: King of Queen' (Manuel Betancourt, 2020). Page 93 from Smooth Radio, 'When Freddie Mercury admitted there was "nothing else left" between him and Queen bandmates' (Thomas Curtis-Horsfall, 2023). Page 94 from Melody Maker, 'The Queen Bee' (Caroline Coon, 1974). Page 95 from NME, 'Interview with Freddie Mercury' (Tony Stewart, 1977). Page 96 from Entertainment Tonight, 'Watch Freddie Mercury's Rare 1982 ET Interview' (2018). Page 97 from Joepie, 'Freddie Mercury Looks Back' (1981). Page 98 from Off The Record (1984). Page 102 from The Daily Mail, 'The last days (and exuberantly wild life) of my friend Freddie Mercury' (David Wigg, 2021). Page 103 from Phonograph Record, 'Queen The New British Invasion' (Mitchell Cohen, 1976). Page 104 from NME, 'Freddie Mercury once told his biographer he felt "imprisoned" by fame' (Sam Moore, 2018). Page 105 from Parade, '75 Freddie Mercury Quotes to Celebrate the 30th Anniversary of the Legendary Freddie Mercury Tribute Concert' (Kai Green, 2022). Page 106 from The Solo Collection: The David Wigg Interviews, 'Ibiza, 1987'. Page 107 from Evening News, 'In the camp of Queen Freddie' (John Blake, 1980). Page 108 from Joepie, 'Mary's Visit Was The Most Beautiful Gift Of All' (1985). Page 109 from 'On Fire: Live At The Bowl' (2004). Page 110 from Vibes, 'Freddie Mercury Rats on Queen' (1977). Page 111 from Record Mirror, 'Blame it on Rio' (Robin Smith, 1985). Page 112 from The Solo Collection: The David Wigg Interviews 'Munich, 1984'. Page 113 from The Solo Collection: The David Wigg Interviews 'Munich, 1984'. Page 114 from The Solo Collection: The David Wigg Interviews, 'Ibiza, 1987'. Page 115 from Hit Parader, 'Queen' (Lester Bangs, 1977). Page 116 from Melody Maker, 'The Queen Bee' (Caroline Coon, 1974). Page 117 from Radio X, 'Brian May reveals Queen have asked John Deacon to rejoin them "a couple of times"' (2022). Page 118 from American Songwriter, 'The 16 Best Freddie Mercury Quotes' (Jacob Utti, 2022).